Get **more** out of libraries

Please return or renew this item by the last date shown.

You can renew online at www.hants.gov.uk/library

Or by phoning   0845 603 5631

Hampshire
County Council

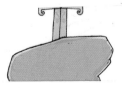

Dear Reader,

There are so many exciting stories about Arthur and Merlin. They've been told many times in new ways over the years. Are they true? We will never know for sure as it all happened so long ago.

My favourite legend is about how Arthur became king by pulling a sword from a stone. It might have happened something like this ...

Julia Golding

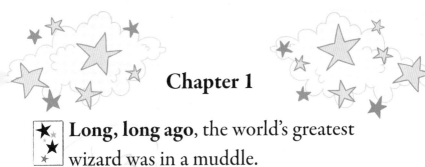

Chapter 1

Long, long ago, the world's greatest wizard was in a muddle.

'Drat!' Merlin shouted.

His pet rat turned purple.

'Help!' he cried.

His rubbish bin exploded and showered him with paper.

'I know I had it somewhere!' moaned Merlin.

Gwen, his niece, skipped into the room carrying a tea tray. She almost dropped it when she saw the mess.

'What's the matter, Uncle Merlin?' she asked.

'It seems,' said Merlin with great dignity, 'that I have lost the King of England.'

'How did you do that?' gasped Gwen.
Merlin blushed.

'You must stop doing this,' she said, wagging her wooden spoon at him. 'Last week it was my cat.'

'Ah, yes,' said Merlin. His cheeks went even pinker.

'You turned poor Tiddles into a fish. It took me ages to find her in the castle moat,' said Gwen.

'I have to practise,' huffed Merlin. 'Thankfully, Tiddles was the only one to swim into my net when I called, "Here, Kitty, Kitty!" Everyone was watching. Do you know how silly I felt?' asked Gwen.

'No,' said Merlin.

'Very!' snapped Gwen.

7

Merlin moved a big blue frog off the table.

'I am sorry about that, my dear,' he said. 'But I will feel even sillier if I have to admit I've lost our future king.'

Gwen poured him a cup of tea.

'Why did you hide him in the first place?' she asked.

'The heir to the throne has many enemies. I wanted him to be safe until we needed him,' said Merlin. 'So I put him away somewhere.'

'Can you not bring him back with a spell?' Gwen asked.

'I would if I could remember his name,' said Merlin. He scratched his head. 'Was it ... Arnold? Adam? Artichoke?'

'I hope not,' Gwen laughed.

'I know! You should set a test that only he can pass and make all the knights take it.'

Merlin clapped his hands.

'Excellent!' he cried. 'I thought I had all the brains in the family, but it seems you have some too.'

'Just a few,' said Gwen. She waved her wooden spoon and cast a secret spell to tidy up his mess.

Chapter 2

Arthur was in the tent preparing the armour for the joust. His foster brother, Sir Kay, came in. He didn't look happy.

'Artie, what have you done to my shield? It's very shiny but it smells of flowers. I can't scare my enemies smelling of violets,' said Sir Kay.

Arthur jumped up and gave the shield a final polish.

'Stop moaning, Kay,' said Arthur. 'I used a new mixture that I made up myself. The old stuff was useless. See, your shield has never looked so good!'

'Humph!' grunted Sir Kay.

'Boys!' called Sir Ector, striding into the tent. 'I have just come from the town. Merlin has set a test for every knight in the land. The winner gets to be king.'

'Can I try?' asked Sir Kay.
'Of course,' said his father.
'And me?' asked Arthur.

Sir Ector put his hand on his foster son's shoulder.

'Artie, you are only a squire,' said Sir Ector. 'You can't take a test like this until you are older.'

Arthur scowled. He felt that he would make a very good king if he was given the chance. He always had lots of ideas. It would be much more fun to have a kingdom in which to try them out.

'Not fair!' he muttered.

'Yes it is,' said Sir Ector. 'Now, please get my weapons ready for the joust this afternoon. Kay and I are off to take the test.'

Left alone in the tent, Arthur polished the armour until it shone like the sun. He couldn't wait to grow up and be a knight. He did a final check on the weapons.

Oh no! Sir Ector's sword was nowhere
to be seen. With a terrible sinking feeling,
Arthur realised that he had used it to stir his
polish mixture. He had left it in the kitchen
at home.

Arthur had to think quickly. He needed another sword – and soon!

He stepped out of the tent and made his way through the camp. It was empty because all the knights were at Merlin's test.

Arthur wondered what the wizard had asked them to do. Fight a dragon? Tame a wild wolf?

When Arthur walked into the town, a big crowd was coming the other way. All the knights were very cross.

'It is impossible!' said Sir Ector.

'Merlin's finally lost his marbles!' exclaimed Sir Kay.

Everyone had failed Merlin's test.

'Let's go and start the joust,' suggested Sir Ector.

'Good idea,' said Sir Kay. 'Are you coming, Artie?'

Arthur shook his head.

'I've got something I have to do first,' he said. 'I won't be long.'

Gwen was feeling sad. Uncle Merlin's clever test had failed. He had enchanted a sword and put it in a stone. Only the true King of England would be able to pull it out. Every knight in the land had tried, but no one had moved it even a tiny bit.

Merlin was sitting on the stone beside her. He was knotting and unknotting his long grey beard, a sure sign that he was upset.

'Are you sure you didn't turn the boy into something else?' suggested Gwen. 'A bird? A flower?'

'No, no. I left him a boy and sent him to stay with some very nice people. I'm just not sure who they were.'

'When I lose something, I try to think where I last saw it,' said Gwen helpfully.

'That's no good,' said Merlin. 'He was a baby lying in a cradle. He won't still be there. That was ten years ago. Or was it twenty? Time passes so quickly when you are as old as I am.'

The two of them watched the young squire walk into the market square. He had his hands tucked in his pockets and he was whistling.

'We'd better vanish,' said Gwen. 'We don't want anyone to see us.'

Merlin waved his wand and they flew up into the nearest tree in the shape of two robins.

Arthur stopped whistling. He couldn't believe his luck. There he was, thinking that he was going to get told off for leaving the sword behind, and lo and behold he had found another one! The only problem was that it seemed to be stuck in a big stone.

Arthur climbed up on a box and took the handle. It came out easily, like a knife out of butter.

Two robins flew out from a nearby tree, twittering excitedly.

Arthur took a quick look round. No one was about to ask if it was all right to borrow the sword. With a shrug, he wrapped it in his cloak and started back for the joust. He had no time to lose.

Chapter 4

'Artie! Where's my sword?' bellowed
Sir Ector.

His opponent, the nasty Sir Grum, was
already swishing his blade to and fro, giving
Sir Ector mean looks.

Arthur jogged on to the field.

'Here!' he said, pushing the new sword into his foster father's hand. 'I couldn't find your old one so I borrowed this.'

Sir Ector's jaw dropped open. Sir Grum fainted and was dragged from the field. The judges awarded the fight to Sir Ector.

'Where did you get this?' Sir Ector asked, ignoring the fuss around him.

'It was a bit weird really,' said Arthur. 'Someone had left it in a stone in the centre of town. I hope they don't mind me taking it.'

'You drew it out yourself?' asked Sir Ector. 'No one helped you?'

'Of course not. It wasn't hard,' said Arthur.

Sir Ector turned to the crowd of knights.

'My foster son, Arthur, is your new king!' he announced.

The knights looked at the sword, then at the boy who claimed to have pulled it from the stone. They laughed.

Sir Kay rushed over, ready to defend his foster brother.

'That was the test and he passed!' he said, raising Arthur's arm in a victory salute.

'We don't believe he did it,' grumbled the knights.

'I'll do it again if you like,' said Arthur. 'I'd rather like to be king, you see.'

Sir Ector and Sir Kay led the way back to the stone.

'There you are, Arthur, you show them,' said Sir Ector.

Arthur took the sword and pushed it into the stone. He stepped back.

'Anyone else want a go?' he asked.

'Me!' said Sir Grum.

He forced his way through the crowd and grabbed the handle.

He heaved, and he heaved, and he heaved. His face went pink, then red, then purple.

'I think you'd better stop,' said Arthur.

Sir Grum let go and said something nasty.

'You do it then,' he growled. 'But I don't believe you can.'

Arthur jumped up on to the stone. He pulled the sword free as if plucking a ripe apple from a tree. He waved it over his head. The knights cheered – all except Sir Grum.

'We can't have a boy as king! This is madness,' he said.

Just then two robins vanished in a flash of light. Merlin and Gwen appeared beside Arthur.

'Where did you come from?' Arthur asked.

Gwen rolled her eyes. 'Uncle lost the spell to make us come back. I had to invent one,' she explained.

Arthur didn't understand magic, but he thought it sounded like fun. He held out his hand.

'I'm Arthur. Pleased to meet you,' he said to Gwen.

Merlin clicked his fingers.

Arthur!

'Arthur! That was the name. I've found him.'

Sir Ector cleared his throat.

'Merlin, we have a problem here. Not everyone wants a boy as their king,' he said.

'Poppycock!' exclaimed Merlin.

Bright red flowers shot out of Sir Grum's helmet.

'Of course Arthur is going to be king. I happen to know he will be the best king this country ever has,' shouted Merlin happily. He did a little dance on the spot.

'Never!' shouted Sir Grum.

Gwen put her hands on her hips and glared at Sir Grum.

'Do you have a problem with that, Sir?' she asked.

'He's a boy!' he said.

'And I'm a girl. But I could still turn you into a beetle if I wanted,' she threatened.

Sir Grum glanced at the wooden spoon tucked in Gwen's apron. It looked a bit like a wand and was shooting golden sparks.

'I've just remembered. I've got to see a man about a dog … a dragon … a something very important,' he spluttered.

Jumping on his horse, Sir Grum made a quick exit.

'Anyone else not want my friend here to be king?' asked Gwen.

There was silence. Arthur grinned. He was already making plans for a special round table. It was time the country had a new order of knights to look after the people.

Merlin rubbed his hands together. 'That's settled then. Now, where did I hide that crown?'